JOKES

from the

Back Seat

Humor for Kids!

JOKES

from the

Back Seat

Humor for Kids!

One-Liners, Puns, Puzzlers, Riddles,
Pirate Jokes, Knock-Knock Jokes,
Tongue-Twisters, and Cartoons

Includes
"Hidden"
Vault

JoBo

WALNUT STREET BOOKS

LANCASTER,
PENNSYLVANIA

Acknowledgments

I want to thank the many people who put up with my dumb jokes.
I apologize to those who heard the same joke over and over and over.

I am especially indebted to my wonderful family--Marilyn, Dan, Morgan,
Ruth, Eric, Luke, and Anna. And to Evie, my favorite sister Lucinda, Lucy,
and Steve for some wonderfully bad jokes. And to Beth and Miguel for
letting me use the dino photo from their wedding.

I also want to thank the Pulitzer Committee for perhaps considering this
book for a prize. And the Nobel Committee. And the MacArthur Foundation.

And you, for buying this book.

Jokes from the Back Seat: Humor for Kids!
Copyright © 2019 by Jay Parrish
All cartoons and artwork copyright © 2019 by Jay Parrish

Softcover International Standard Book Number: 9781947597143
PDF: 9781947597150
EPUB: 9781947597167
Kindle: 9781947597174
Library of Congress Control Number: Data available

Cover Design by Mike Bond and Cliff Snyder
Design by Cliff Snyder

Jokes from the Back Seat: Humor for Kids! is published
by Walnut Street Books, Lancaster, Pennsylvania

info@walnutstreetbooks.com

Table of Contents

"It's so hard to get applause on T. Rex night."

THREE IMPORTANT NOTES—
(_before_ you read this book)

1. If you find a joke with a small "V" and a number, such as "V12," that indicates that you can go to "The VAULT" at the back of this book (the upside-down pages), beginning on page 127.

In The VAULT, you will find additional information about that joke, including what might make it funny. For example:

What do you call a fake noodle?

An impasta. V6

If you go The VAULT and look for V6, it will say:

V6: An "imposter" is someone who pretends to be something they're not. Noodles are a form of pasta. "Impasta" sounds like "imposter."

2. There are 10 pages in this book that you'll need to read with the help of a mirror.

These are pages 24, 25, 32, 33, 48, 49, 72, 73, 106, and 107. Just hold them to a mirror to read!

3. Some pages are upside down. To read them, stand on your head!

Some Jokes

It was so cold in the barn that the cows gave ice cream.

Dogs can't take X-rays, but cat scan.

Q: What do you find on a tiny beach?
A: Microwaves.

I would tell you the "288 joke," but it's too gross. v1

A woman walked into a doctor's office with food smeared all over her face and vegetables stuck in her hair. The doctor said, "I can see you're not eating well."

A cockroach left his home from behind the refrigerator and went west. Now he has a home on the range. v2

You can't weather a tree, but you can climate.

Q: What did one eye say to the other?
A: Between you and me, something smells.

I like elevator jokes... They work on so many levels.

I'm so good at sleeping that I can do it with my eyes closed.

"Say, 'People!'"

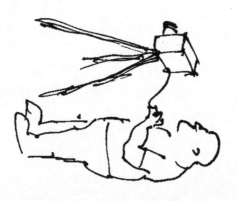

The home appliance store hired a chicken as a salesperson. After a few weeks, they found they were losing money. It turns out it was a free-range chicken.

The Mona Lisa was accused of theft. But the police thought she was framed. v3

Atom1: "I think I'm missing an electron."
Atom 2: "Are you sure?"
Atom 1: "I'm positive." v4

A suburban farmer gave up raising chickens because he felt cooped up.

A mechanic came into a doctor's office and said, "Last night I dreamed I was a muffler, and I woke up exhausted."

Q: How lonely were you?
A: I was so lonely I played dodgeball with myself.
I usually lost.

Tom: What is 3,000 in Roman numerals?
Sue: "Mmm..."
Tom: "Right!" v5

Q: What do you call a fake noodle?
A: An impasta. v6

A baby skunk was lost far into the woods. He
wandered all night and finally made it home.
His surprised mother asked how he did it.
He said, "Instinct." v7

They say money talks.
Mine just says goodbye.

Q: Why do cows have hooves?
A: They lactose. v8

Q: What does a panda use to fry hamburgers?
A: A pan. Duh.

A botanist enjoyed his work with
mushrooms. He told friends he
was lichen it. And, of course, he
was a fungi. v9

The local pond has strict rules. Only frogs are
allowed. All others will be toad. v10

A thesaurus has "synonym rolls" for breakfast.

How many dogs in a pound?

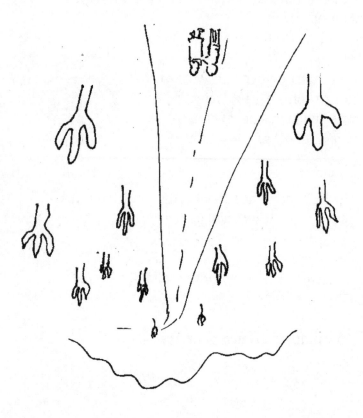

They all seem so happy to see us!

Q: Why can't crabs and lobsters be more generous?
A: They're shellfish.

Q: How did the popular kid burn his mouth?
A: He took a bite of his pizza before it was cool.

A thief walked into a store.
"Ouch!" he said.

A mime was arrested and told he had the right to remain silent. V11

The bread sat all day and didn't rise. But then at 2 a.m., it did! When you yeast expect it...

Q: What do you call a hippie's wife?
A: Mississippi.

Abraham Lincoln was so tall his feet barely reached the ground. V12

A very loud frog said, "I'M A VERY LOUD FROG. WHAT ARE YOU?"

"I'm a heron."

"THAT'S NICE. I LIKE TO EAT BUGS. WHAT DO YOU EAT?"

"Loud frogs."

"....oh, really?"

In a city run by crabs, there are only sidewalks. v13

Q: What's the best thing about Switzerland?
A: Its flag is a plus.

I visited the Air and Space Museum. There was nothing there. v14

The builder put the top on the house, weeks after the rest was done. S'late roof.

Q: What does Mabel the Jungle Cow swing on?
A: A bovine. v15

On a cold day, Luke heard that it was even-side-of-the-street plowing, and everyone should move their cars to the odd side. So he moved his car.

The next night, they said it was odd-side-of-the-street plowing. So he moved the car to the even side of the street.

The third night it snowed again and he said, "Enough! I'm leaving my car in the garage."

A talented young man was working in the wheat field with his father when the combine ripped his father's hand clear off.

Thinking quickly, the son reattached the hand and got him to the hospital.

The doctors at the hospital were so impressed that they got the young man into the local medical school.

On the first day of classes, his father went with him and met the dean of the school, who said, "You must be very proud of your son."

The father reached out his hands with thumbs extended and exclaimed proudly, "He's great!" V16

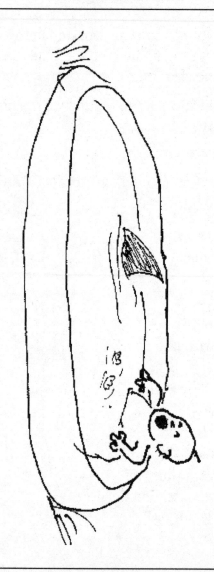

"Dad! I think it's time to clean the pool again!"

The Spanish magician asked his audience to count to three and he would disappear.

They chanted, "Uno!...Dos!..."

But then he vanished without a Tres. v17

They aren't making yardsticks any longer. v 18

A major league baseball team hired an orchestra conductor to give the play-by-play because he always knew the score. v19

The view at the seashore was breath-taking and outstanding.

In fact, it was without pier. v20

An asteroid befriended a smaller celestial object, bound for the earth.

They became good friends, even though the asteroid was vegetarian and the celestial object was a little meteor. V21

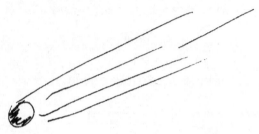

If you believe in telekinesis, raise my hand. V22

"Well, to be frank...
I'd have to change my name."

Luke had faithful dog who went with him everywhere. The dog also wore a stethoscope around his neck.

Anna asked, "What's with the stethoscope?"

And Luke said, "I sent him to the wrong school, and now all he can do is heal." v23

(You need a mirror.)

"I just found this part.
Let's just assume it's not important."

A visitor checked into a New York hotel.

The manager said, "We have breakfast from 6-10, lunch from 10-2 and dinner from 2-10."

The visitor asked, "When am I supposed to do any sightseeing?"

Jimmy carried a piano with him in case he got locked out. Because a piano has 88 keys.

Did you hear about the corduroy pillow?
It's making headlines.

Q: How does a cow relax?
A: It watches a Mooooovie.

Riddles

Q: Which side of a pelican has the most feathers?
A: The outside.

Q: What does a pig put on a burn?
A: Oinkment.

Q: Why was the math book sad?
A: It had lots of problems.

Q: Why did the boy eat his homework?
A: Because his teacher said it was "a piece of cake."

Q: What's the biggest store in China?
A: The Great Wall Mart.

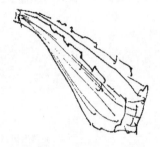

Q: What did one snowman say to the other?
A: "Do you smell carrots?"

Q: What did Batman say to Robin before they got into the car?
A: "Get into the car."

Q: What does a duck say when buying Chapstick?
A: "Put it on my bill."

Q: Why did the stream feel sad?
A: It's future was all downhill.

Q: What do skunks sit on in church?
A: Pews. V24

Q: What has four wheels and flies?
A: A garbage truck.

Q: What word has only one letter in it?
A: Envelope.

Q: Why didn't the skeleton go to the dance?
A: He had noBODY to go with.

Q: Why did the girl stop using her pencil?
A: It was pointless.

Q: Why can't you trust atoms?
A: Because they make up literally everything.

Q: What's large, grey, and doesn't matter?
A: An irrelephant.

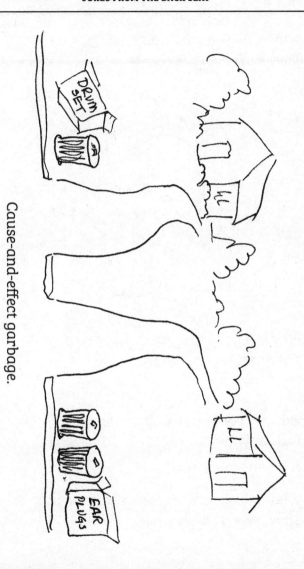

Cause-and-effect garbage.

Q: Why don't you see whales hiding in trees?
A: They can't climb. v25

Q: Why is it good to travel with an elephant?
A: They bring their own trunk. v26

Q: How far can you walk into the forest?
A: Half way.

Q: What makes golf course websites so useful?
A: They have a lot of links.

Q: What's your favorite planetary music?
A: Neptune.

Q: What animal always attends a wedding?
A: The ring bear-er.

Q: Why are leopards good at standing in lines?
A: They never lose their spots.

Q: What do you call four string quartets?
A: A gallon of music.

(You need a mirror.)

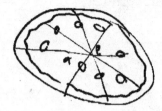

Q: Why did the pizza not like the low-budget horror movie?
A: It was too cheesy.

Q: Why was the Moon misbehaving?
A: It was going through a phase. v27

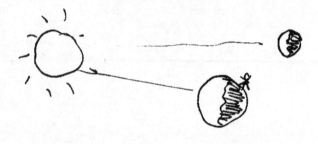

Q: Why did the Australian bear not get the job he applied for?
A: He didn't have the koalifications.

Q: Why did an electrician subscribe to an electronics magazine?
A: He wanted to keep current. v28

Q: What do you call an animal with no eyes?
A: Anmal.

Q: Where did the omelet go
when the kitchen caught fire?
A: Out the eggs-it. rev

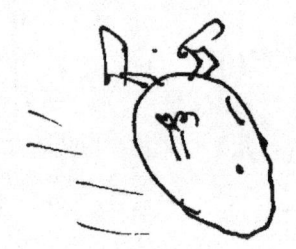

Q: What do you call a restaurant in Canada?
A: A buff-eh? rev

Q: What do you call a cow eating grass?
A: A lawn Mooooower.

Q: What time do you go to the dentist?
A: Tooth hurty. rev

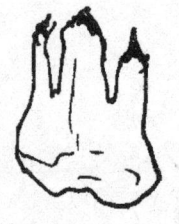

Shhhh! The field has ears!

Q: Why shouldn't you ask for a ride from a cow?
A: They're always going the udder way.

Q: What happens if you tend your garden while barefoot?
A: You may end up with toe-ma-toes.

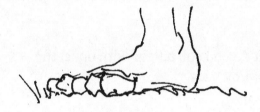

Q: What's a Scottish duck-billed aquatic mammal called?
A: A plaidypus. v32

Q: Why are the restaurants on the moon so unpopular?
A: They have no atmosphere.

Q: How do you get down off an elephant?
A: You don't. You get down off a goose. v33

Q: Why did a farmer raise her vegetables in an old row boat?
A: Because she wanted them to be oar-ganic.

Q: What do you call a bear with no teeth?
A: A gummy bear.

Q: Why do you invite bread dough to a social event?
A: It always rises to the occasion.

Q: Why didn't the ball roll downhill?
A: It wasn't inclined.

Q: Why can't you believe the animals you hear in the jungle?
A: One of them might be a lion.

Q: How do you measure how high your grass is?
A: With a yardstick. v34

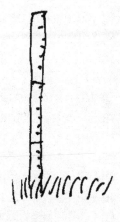

Q: What do you call the grandmother of a yellow fruit?
A: Banana nana.

BIG BOX STORE

Q: What's the past tense of "Sitern"?
A. Saturn.

Q: Why was a sugar farmer always causing trouble?
A: He raised cane. V35

Q: What's black and white and red all over?
A: That's easy. A newspaper.
Q: OK, let me ask again. What's black and white and red all over?
A: A sunburned zebra.

"Love your outfit."

Q: What's a metaphor?
A: It's so cows have a place to graze. v36

Q: What do people call a bug in a Boston jail?
A: A cell tick.

Q: What kind of tree fits in your hand?
A: A palm tree!

Q: Why are cows good in a traffic jam?
A: They know how to use their horns.

Q: What do you call a young sapling?
A: An infantry.

Q: What does the moon do with its toenails?
A: Eclipse them.

Q: Why don't you want to be tickled by an octopus?
A: Because they have tentacles. V37

Q: What did the band leader use to brush her teeth?
A: Tubapaste.

Q: What do you call a snowman on a summer vacation?
A: Water.

Q: Who is Old Man River married to?
A: Mrs. Sippi.

Q: Name a color, followed by a letter making a food that you can eat—
A: Green "p," Brown "e," Green "t." And don't forget the Buff "a." V38

Q: What do you call a cat at the beach at Christmas?
A: Sandy Paws.

Q: What did 0 say to 8?
A: Hey, nice belt!

Q: What has one head, one foot and four legs?
A: A bed.

Q: How many months have 28 days?
A: All of them.

Q: What song do the fish in "South Pacific" sing?
A: Salmon Enchanted Evening.

Q: How did the tree excuse itself from a Spring dinner at Old Man Winter's?
A: Sorry, but I have to leaf now.

Q: Why did the baker make a lot of bread?
A: He kneaded the dough.

Q: Why did the chicken cross the road twice?
A: She was a double-crosser.

Q: What ingredients do you use to make a solitary salad?
A: Lettuce alone.

Q: What is the name of a large southeastern Asian ship that sank?
A. Thai-tanic.

Q: What did the momma cow say to the baby cow?
A: It's pasture bedtime.

Q: What's the difference between a hippo and a Zippo?
A: One's very heavy, and the other is a little lighter.

"My mother collects art. She's a dentist."

Q: Why did the cold shopper go into the bookstore?
A: To get between some covers.

Q: Why were the dictatorial doves worried?
A: Because the pigeons wanted to stage a coo. V39

Q: What can't you spell "llama" on Christmas?
A: There's Noel.

Q: What did the magician fisherman say?
A: Pick a cod, any cod.

Q: What has only seven letters but is also filled with letters?
A: Mailbox.

Q: How do you find out what a turkey is saying?
A: You Google "gobble."

Q: Why, when a flight of geese goes overhead, is one arm of the V longer than the other?
A: More geese.

Q: Why do people like Sunday?
A: The day before was a sadder day.

Q: What is red and smells like blue paint?
A: Red paint.

Man to lawyer: What do you charge?
Lawyer: $1,000 for 3 questions.
Man: Isn't that awfully expensive?
Lawyer: Yes. What's your last question?

Q: Why does Santa have three gardens at the North Pole?
A: So he can Ho Ho Ho.

Q: What do Alexander the Great and Winnie the Pooh have in common?
A: Same middle name.

Knock-Knock Jokes

Dan: Knock knock.
Jan: Who's there?
Dan: Mister.
Jan: Mister who?
Dan: Mister a lot, when my sister was on vacation.

Jen: Knock knock.
Jon: Who's there?
Jen: Flounder.
Jon: Flounder who?
Jen: She flounder umbrella that was missing.

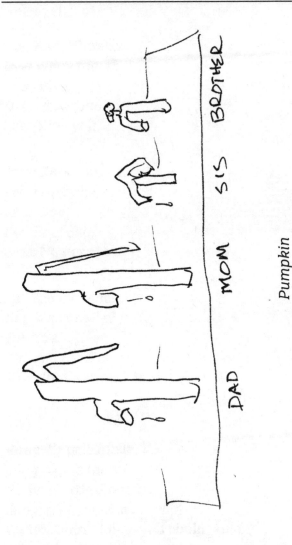

Pumpkin

(You need a mirror.)

Lee: Knock Knock.
Dee: Who's there?
Lee: Olive.
Dee: Olive who?
Lee: Olive you.

Jess: Knock knock.
Les: Who's there?
Jess: Boo!
Les: Boo who?
Jess: No need to cry.

Jill: Knock knock.
Bill: Who's there?
Jill: Yah.
Bill: Yah who?
Jill: What's so exciting?

Rudy: Knock knock.
Judy: Who's there?
Rudy: A little old lady.
Judy: A little old lady who?
Rudy: I didn't know you could yodel.

Pat: Knock, knock.

Matt: Who's there?

Pat: Fortification.

Matt: Fortification who?

Pat: Fortification we're going to Disneyland!

Brian: Knock knock.

Ryan: Who's there?

Brian: Utah.

Ryan: Utah who?

Brian: Utah, I'm short.

Ben: Knock knock.

Jen: Who's there?

Ben: Isabel.

Jen: Isabel who?

Ben: Why are you knocking, Isabel not working?

Jay: Knock knock.

Ray: Who's there?

Jay: Say.

Ray: Say who?

Jay: Who.

Trace: Knock knock.
Grace: Who's there?
Trace: Omelet.
Grace: Omelet who?
Trace: Omelet smarter than I look.

Sue: Knock knock.
Drew: Who's there?
Sue: Mini.
Drew: Mini who?
Sue: Minisoda.

Jim: Knock knock.
Mim: Who's there?
Jim: Cash.
Jim: Cash who?
Mim: No thanks, I don't like nuts.

Jenny: Knock knock.
Renny: Who's there?
Jenny: Deja.
Renny: Deja who?
Jenny: Knock knock.

Medium rare? No, no. They all come out well done.

Cam: Knock knock.
Sam: Who's there?
Cam: A psychic.
Sam: A psychic who?
Cam: I knew you were going to say that.

Perry: You can't do a Fourth-of-July knock-knock joke.
Mary: Why?
Perry: Because Freedom rings.

Mindy: Knock knock.
Cindy: Who's there?
Mindy: Sally sometimes sells shiny seashells by the seashore.
Cindy: Sally sometimes sells shiny seashells by the seashore who?
Mindy: Wow, you don't do alliteration well, do you? V40

Stu: Knock knock.
Sue: Who's there?
Stu: Banana.
Sue: Banana who?
Stu: Banana banana.
Sue: Banana banana who?
Stu: Banana banana banana.
Sue: Banana banana banana who?
Stu: Orange.
Sue: Orange who?
Stu: Aren't you glad I didn't say banana?!

Nell: Knock knock.
Neal: Who's there?
Nell: Wilbur Wright.
Neal: Wilbur Wright back after this commercial.

Bess: Knock knock.
Tess: Who's there?
Bess: Saul.
Jess: Saul who?
Tess: Saul there is.

Brain Teasers

Stare at the center of this drawing. How many gray dots are there? V41

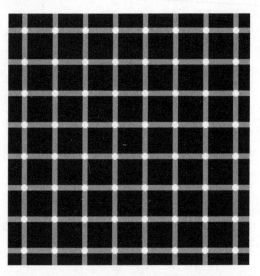

What has four letters, sometimes has seven letters, never has five letters and always has six? V42

Q: Anna's mother had four children: Eeenie, Meanie, Minnie and _____?
A: Anna.

Q: Anna told Luke she could come up with a song with the name of anyone he could think of. Luke thought for a while and suggested Bernie Bontrager. To his surprise she sang a song with that name! What was the song?
A: Happy Birthday.

Q: Which word is misspelled in the dictionary?
A: Misspelled.

Q: What can never be put in a pan?
A: Its lid.

Q: What's orange and sounds like a ferret?
A: A carrot.

Q: On what day of the year are the fewest people born?
A: February 29.

Q: Name three sequential days without using Monday, Tuesday, Wednesday, Thursday, or Friday.
A: Yesterday, Today, Tomorrow.

Q: What goes up when the rain comes down?
A: An umbrella.

Q: What is the longest word in the dictionary?
A: "Smiles," because there's a mile between each "s."

Q: What weighs more—a pound of rocks or a pound of feathers?
A: They weigh the same.

Q: Poor people have it. Rich people need it. If you eat it, you die. What is it?
A: Nothing.

"*There's something ominous about the moon tonight.*"

More Humor and Jokes

A stallion asked a pony why it wasn't talking, and the pony said, "I'm a little horse." V43

A photon came into a store and the clerk said, "Why are you carrying such a small suitcase?"

And the photon said, "Because I'm travelling light." V44

They canceled the psychics' meeting but didn't tell anyone because they figured they'd all know in advance. V45

A woman wore fruit shoes. She had them fixed at a cheery cobbler.

A small footstool said, "I never knew my real dad, only my stepladder."

A trouble-making baker was hired at a boring bakery because they hoped he would stir things up.

I like the clown who held the door for me...I thought it was a nice jester.

A scientist spilled spot remover on his dog, and now it's invisible.

Bob was so unfortunate. He was once locked in his convertible without the keys. And it was raining! And the roof was down!

The next week he was stuck on an escalator for hours.

And yesterday he was putting siding on his house and he hurt his thumb hammering because the head of the nail was on the wrong end. His smarter sister, Lisa, said, "Don't worry, we can use the defective nails on the other side of the house."

There once was a soccer fan who went to Disneyland. He stood in line for hours to get on rides. Finally he got on the Mad Tea Party ride. He was thrilled. "At last," he exclaimed, "I'll be in the Whirled Cup!" V46

You can always know how much a fish weighs because they carry their own scales.

There once was a world-famous knot expert. He was an amateur. V47

"Honey, I'm afraid Junior is just going to be a couch potato."

Two llamas prepared to take a hike. One said, "Alpaca lunch." V48

They made the new orchestra hall using mostly tuba fours.

The carpenter took so long they called him Fermata. V49

A boy was on his first plane ride. He eagerly looked out the window and occasionally made an "X" on the armrest with a pencil.

His seatmate asked, "What are you doing?"

"Every time I see something interesting, I mark down where we are, so I can see it on the way back."

"What if the earth moves while we're away from the plane?"

"Oh, I hadn't thought of that. And worse still, what if we don't get the same plane?" V50

Bill: "I'm giving up fly fishing."
Sara: "Why?
Bill: "You can only eat so many flies."

A vegetable farmer planted his crops using lots of fertilizer. He wanted his celery to be high. V51

The building manager hired a flight of steps to be the night watchman for his building, because he knew they could stair well.

Anna swallowed a dictionary whole and now she has thesaurus throat.

Nomads are known to be in tents. [Say it out loud.] V52

A cobbler decided to run for president. He figured he was a shoe-in.

When she was done with her bike she placed it in the recycle bin.

If attacked by clowns, go for the juggler. v53

Some scientists tried a newly developed clown-flavored ice cream. But it tasted funny.

Dairies along the San Andreas fault provide straight-from-the-cow milkshakes.

I told my friend 10 jokes to try to make him laugh. Sadly, no pun in 10 did.

Q: How many dogs can fit in your car?
A: Six.
Q: How many people can fit in your car?
A: None, it's full of dogs.

"It just gives me the creeps—all those eyes."

George: "How lonely were you?"
Jill: "I was so lonely that I made dinner reservations for two, and then didn't show up."

My eye doctor fell into his lens grinder and made a spectacle of himself.

Q: What's this?
\/
A: A dead one of these—
/\   V54

A well-meaning woman gave a young musician some poorly baked cookies.

The musician tried them, but they tasted so bad that he couldn't eat them. So he threw them out in the backyard where birds eagerly ate them.

When he met the woman the next time, she asked how the cookies were. He replied, "They were eaten and enjoyed." V55

MEET THE SPOONASAURUS!

Here is Spoonasaurus in his natural habitat, eating cake.

Be on the lookout the next time you eat anything. Spoonasaurus may try to take it from you!

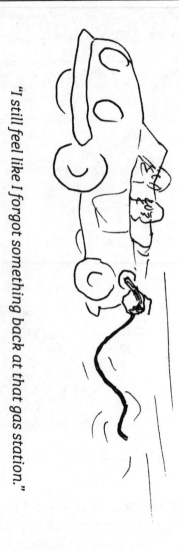

"I still feel like I forgot something back at that gas station."

A small family invited a guest for dinner.

After dinner, they sat back and, one after another, would say a random number. And everyone would laugh.

The guest was puzzled and asked what was so funny. They said, "We have all heard all our jokes so many times that we just say the number and we remember that joke."

Trying to fit in the guest said, "13". But no one laughed.

The father leaned over and said, "You really didn't tell it very well."

The guest, in desperation, said, "12,945," and everyone broke into laughter.

The mother said, "We never heard that one before!" V56

A patron came to the help desk of the library and asked for a 1:1 map of the world. The librarian replied, "You're standing on it." V57

A list of three things that are invisible:
1.
2.
3.

Jon: Why did the chicken cross the road?

Don: That's easy. To get to the other side.

Jon: OK, you're so smart. Why did the turkey NOT cross the road?

Don: I don't know.

Jon: He was a big chicken. V58

There once was a plot of land that a city set aside for retiring cows. The cows would kick off their shoes, line them up on a rack, and relax in the grass for the rest of their lives.

It was called "Moo Shoe Park." V59

They wanted to sweeten the movie by putting cinema sugar on it. V60

The hopeful rabbit was nervous and short of breath as he gave his girlfriend a 20-carrot ring.

There was a criminal who murdered people with boxes of Chocolate Covered Sugar Stars. He was a cereal killer.

A man came into the Memphis library and asked where the furthest city in the world from Memphis was. The librarian replied, "If you start driving east, that would be West Memphis." V61

(You need a mirror.)

A pan of muffins was in an oven. One muffin turned to another muffin and said, "Is it my imagination or is it getting warm in here?" The other muffin said, "What? A talking muffin?!"

I was having such a hard day that, when I sat in my dressing room and tried to put my head in my hands, I missed.

A spice salesman had good quality goods and lower quality ones. He had the best of thymes and the worst of thymes.

Last night I slept like a baby. I woke up every two hours and cried.

The wedding was so beautiful that even the cake was in tiers.

A Hawaiian tourist walked into a Taco Bell in Dallas and ordered a frito lei. véz

What is the tallest building in town?
The library—it has so many stories.

A retired astronomer said he didn't find his job weighing on him after all. It was a light year.

Looking out her window, Anna saw two men in the park. One dug a hole. They'd stand and talk a little, and then the second would fill it in. Then they'd walk about 20 feet away and do it again. Anna went out to talk with them.

"Why do you dig a hole and then just fill it in?" she asked.

The first man said, "We are part of a three-man team. We plant trees. I dig the hole. Bob plants the tree. And then Joe, here, fills in the dirt. Bob is sick today."

"Quicksand's a myth," you said.

"No, I googled it," I said. "It's a real thing."

"Who you going to believe? Me or Google?" you said.

"Do we have time — I'm being pulled down — to google it again?"

What do we want?

What do we want?
Hearing aids!
When do we want it?
Hearing aids! V63

What do we want?
Procrastination!
When do we want it?
Later! V64

What do we want?
Time travel!
When do we want it?
It doesn't matter! V65

What do we want?
A bathroom stop!
When do want it?
Before it doesn't matter! V66

What do we want?
Spices!
When do we want them?
Any Thyme!

What do we want?
A break from eating!
When do we want it?
Fast! V67

What do we want?
To go to Disney World!
When do we want to go?
Before it becomes Sea World! V68

What do we want?
Punch lines!
When do we want them?
Right about now!

What do we want?
Relativistic speed!
When do want it?
It depends!

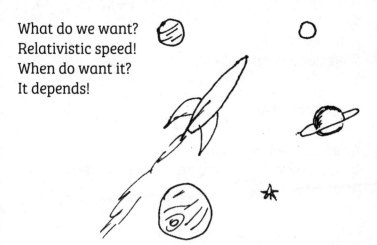

What do we want?
Measures of electrical power!
Watt?

What do we want?
Chicken-crossing-the-road jokes!
Why do we want them?
To get to the other side.

What do we want?
Silence!
When do we want it?
(Don't say anything!) V69

What do we want?
Synonyms!
When do we want them?
Quickly, soon, fast, in the near future, presently,
rapidly. V70

What do we want?
Asparagus!
Why do we want it?
Because we only have one a-gus! V71

Words of Wisdom

You can tuna piano but you can't piano a tuna.

Tweet others as you would have others tweet you.

Never run with bagpipes, you might get kilt. V72

If you think you are too small to be effective, you have never been in the dark with a mosquito. V73

Two wrongs don't make a right—but three left turns do.

Some cause happiness wherever they go; others whenever they go. V74

Always remember you're unique. Just like everyone else.

I feel more like I do now than when I first came in. V75

Bread rises in the yeast and sets on the waist. V76

Be alert. The world needs more lerts. V77

Pirate Jokes

Q: What kind of fruit does a pirate like?
A: An ARRRange.

Q: Favorite cheese?
A: ChedARRR.

Q: What's a pirate's favorite letter?
A: ARRRRRR.

Knock knock.
Who's there?
Pirate.
Pirate who?
ARRRRnge you glad I didn't say banana?

When hurt, a pirate goes to an E ARRRR. v78

Q: How much does a pirate pay for his earrings?
A: A buck an ear. v79

Q: What's a pirate's favorite letter?
A: ARRRRR.
A: No he loves the C.

Q: What country do pirates come from?
A: ARRRRgentina.

Q: What does a Pirate look at all day?
A: His Ayye phone.

Q: Who designed the Pirate Museum?
A: An ARRRchitect.

Q: What state do pirates come from?
A: ARRRkansas.

Q: What does a pirate get his wife for Christmas?
A: A pARRRRtridge in a pear tree.

Q: What did the pirate see in Paris?
A: The Ayeeful Tower.

Q: What do land pirates drive?
A: A cARRRRRRR.

Q: What's a pirate electronics museum?
A: VCRrrrr.

Rokes and Jiddles

These next few stories must be read aloud.

Here's how it works. You take adjacent words and exchange their first letters. Sometime you may have to take the first two letters if it's a digraph like "sh" or "ch."

For example:

Once upon a time there was a fairy godmother who gave an enchanted pumpkin to a young woman.

Becomes:

Unce opon a time where tas a gairy fodmother gho wave a penchanted eumpkin to a woung yoman.

Her came was Ninderella. She was boung and yeautiful. And had strong, laight hair. He shad a stevil epmother and mriendly fice. And a shoose loe. But the prandsome Hince hound fer and they hived lappily aver efter.

Or

I drike living in cur oar. The pun feople in the sont freat lan caugh at the rokes and jiddles te well in the sack beat. Apon urrival at our dinal festination we will weep slell.

Why chid the dicken ross the croad?
To tet go the ser othide.

Jond, Bames Jond.

Old Hother Mubberd
She cent to the wubbard
To petch her foor bog a done.
But shen whe thot gere
The bubbard was care,
And so the door pog nad hone.

Rittle Led Hiding Rood took a gasket of boodies to her wandmother in the groods. The Big Wad Bolf was hiding in her bandmother's gred. "Why mat eig byes you have!" said Rittle Led Hiding Rood.

"The setter to bee you with!" said the Big Wad Bolf.

"My, what a mig bouth you have!" said Rittle Led Hiding Rood.

"The eetter to bat you with!" said the Big Wad Bolf.

Then Rittle Led Hiding Rood jold a toke that fas so wunny that the wolf lied daughing. And she hived lappily aver efter.

Exast lit tefore boll.

Gike a lood steighbor nate tharm is fere.

A brop in the ducket.

A fenny por hour youghts.

A thones strow.

Flime ties rike a larrow.

A mool and his foney are poon sarted.

Rools fush in aere whgels trear to fead.

Ly and barge.

Wock on knood.

"Maybe next year we should get an artificial tree."

Yenever whou yind fou ore an the mide of the sajority, it is pime to tauise rend aflect.

—Twark Main

Whose tho rannot cemember the cast are pondemned ro tepeat it.

—Seorge Gantayana

Wenny pise and found poolish.

Brack your rains.

Raining dats and cogs.

The chig beese.

Thood gings thome to cose wat thait.

Prownie boints.

Though of enat!

Write your own: V80

"Cross my heart and hope to die."

Becomes: _____

_____

"The early bird catches the worm."

Becomes: _____

_____

"Children should be seen and not heard."

Becomes: _____

_____

"The darkest hour is just before dawn."

Becomes: _____

_____

"To boldly go where no man has gone before."

Becomes: _____

_____

"A picture is worth a thousand words."

Becomes: _____

_____

"A nest of vipers."

Becomes: _____

"A rolling stone gathers no moss."

Becomes: _____

_____

"A dog is a man's best friend."

Becomes: _____

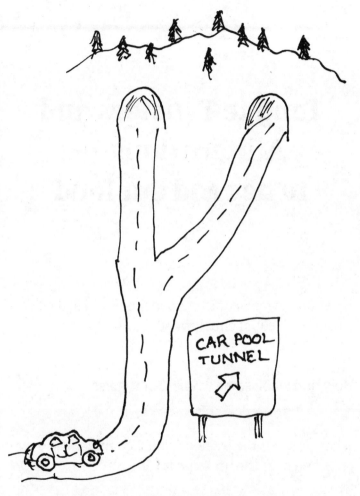

"*Don't turn off — it looks painful.*"

Tongue Twisters and Alliterations— to be read out loud

How much wood could a woodchuck chuck if a woodchuck could chuck wood?

Holy and wholesome whole donut holes.

When you exit the freeway, you'll go under the overpass and over the underpass.

Frankly, Freddy's frequent fascination with Frieda's fetching fragrance frustrated Freddy's fragmentary frivolity.

Andy Abernathy was always an affiliate of the American Anti-Alliteration Association of America.

Barry baked Baby Biscuit bars.

And commonly called cousins and comrades.

 Dreaming donut dunkers don't deny devouring delicious dumplings or delectable Dorito dips.

Even though every éclair ends up eaten eventually.

A French fryer flipped fromage and franks at a friendly fair for free.

Gigantic gooey garbage globs glow green and grind growing gardenias into the ground.

Hard, heavy hazelnuts are hurled with Herculean hefting, by Henry Higgenbottom.

Try making your own alliterative sentences... ask each person to add one sentence using the next letter.

For example, if you begin each of your words (or nearly every word) with the letter "s," the next person should begin each word (or nearly every word) with the letter "t."

Quiet quirky Quakers are quite the quality quilters.

Really rough radishes are red and raspy relatives of raspberry ruffians.

There was a young lady named Bright
Whose speed was far faster than light;
She set out one day
In a relative way
And returned on the previous night. V81

Betty Botta bought a bit of butter;
"But," she said, "this butter's bitter!
If I put it in my batter
It will make my batter bitter.
But a bit o' better butter
Will make my batter better."
Then she bought a bit o' butter
Better than the bitter butter.
Made her bitter batter better.
So 'twas better Betty Botta
Bought a bit o' better butter. V82

Esau Woods' wood-saw would saw wood faster
than any wood-saw that Esau Wood saw saw
wood would saw wood.

CHUBBY KNUCKLES

There once was an ice cream vendor in Ann Arbor, Michigan, who gave change using his own names for coins. Try it and see if you like it. Say it out loud.

5 cents – chubby knuckle

10 cents – deemer

25 cents – qweeter

Dollar – dooler

$1.65 is one dooler, two qweeters, a deemer, and a chubby knuckle.

Now ask the people for various amounts of money before the next rest stop. For example, say, "Hey, could I please have two qweeters, a deemer, and a chubby knuckle?"

And when you buy something in a store, count the change you get back out loud, and watch the cashier's face!

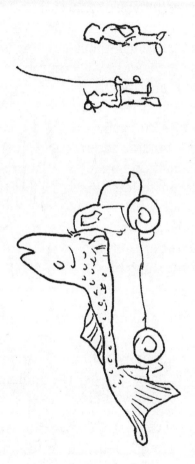

"I only caught one today."

JOHNNY WHOOP

Ask the audience (maybe of one) to pay close attention so they can repeat it. Hold up one hand and touch the tip of each finger, starting with your pinky and working toward your thumb, saying, "Johnny" as you touch each fingertip. Then, when you get to the index finger, run your finger down the outside edge of your index finger and up to then inside of your thumb to its tip, saying, "Whoop!" as you do this, and then "Johnny" when you touch your thumb. Then do the same thing in reverse.

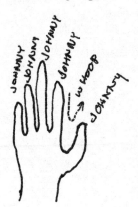

So you say, "Johnny, Johnny, Johnny, Johnny, Whoop, Johnny, Johnny, Whoop, Johnny, Johnny, Johnny, Johnny." Then fold your arms and ask the audience to do what you did.

After a try or two they'll get the finger pointing and Johnny parts right, but rarely will they fold their arms. They'll focus on the fingers and Johnny's but stop paying attention once you finish and not notice the arm crossing. Be generous in doing the Johnny Whoop thing. The longer it goes, the more fun when they figure it out.

Bob ran away from home, then turned left and ran the same distance, turned left and ran the same distance and then left and the same distance. He was back home. Why did everyone cheer? V83

Herb, who was Polish, was an august professional polisher, but got a new job picking herbs for Job in August. V84

WHAT PATTERN IS REPRESENTED BY THESE LETTERS? V85

OTTFFSSENT
ETTFFSSENT

Van Gogh was an excellent getaway driver. He kept his car in good condition, no nut was Toulouse.

He stole a lot of Monet. He could really step on Degas and go down the Rodin escape.

And he was funny. It Cezanne his tombstone, "Vincent Van Gogh, No one is Whittier." V86

Sometimes words just sound funny

Cattywampus - askew

Lollygag – falling behind

Brouhaha – uproar, fight

Hinky - dishonest

Argle-bargle – copious but meaningless talk or writing; it can be a noun or used as an adverb, as in "I did a lot of argle-bargling in class today."

Snollygoster – unprincipled person

Mumbo-jumbo – meaningless language

Mumpsimus – a tradition that continues even after it's been shown to be unreasonable.

Now all these words do you no good if you don't use them in sentences. Think up an entire conversation with the people in the front seat using all the words you've learned.

"My books back here are all cattywampus."

"My brother is starting a brouhaha."
(This is particularly useful if you say it slowly, by syllables—"brou-ha-ha." And then just emphasize the last two "ha ha.")

"Did you think the cashier at the rest stop was acting a little hinky?"

"Are you tired of my argle-bargle?"

And in Finnish the word for a soapstone vendor is *saippuakivikauppias.* Try saying that. Then say it backwards! v87

"So that's what an engineer looks like?"

(You need a mirror.)

Mark Twain Repeatables

"Training is everything. The peach was once a bitter almond; cauliflower is nothing but cabbage with a college education."

"The reports of my death have been greatly exaggerated."

"It is better to keep your mouth closed and let people think you are a fool than to open it and remove all doubt."

"A lie can travel halfway around the world while the truth is putting on its shoes."

"A clear conscience is the sure sign of a bad memory."

"Wagner's music is better than it sounds."

"Clothes make the man. Naked people have little or no influence on society."

"Always do what is right. It will gratify half of mankind and astound the other."

"Never put off till tomorrow what you can do the day after tomorrow."

"Part of the secret of a success in life is to eat what you like and let the food fight it out inside."

"When in doubt, tell the truth."

"Let us endeavor so to live so that when we come to die even the undertaker will be sorry."

Riddles for you to ask persons in the Front Seat —or any adults

Q: Why did the chicken cross the road?
A: To receive a Pullet Surprise. v88

A famous hog was also a mathematician. Did he deal with a porcine or with cosines? v89

A policewoman raided a restaurant and took food away as evidence. She approached a customer and said, "I'm sorry but I have to seize your salad." v90

Q: A gingerbread man came out of the oven with a bad knee. When he went to the doctor, what do you think the doctor said?

A: "Have you tried icing it?"

Let's do a knock-knock joke.
You start. v91

Q: Where did the small appliance go for vacation?
A: Hamilton Beach.

Knock, knock.
Who's there?
Henry David.
Henry David who?
Henry David, Thoreau the ball to me! v92

Luke's pet parrot was obnoxious. After much complaining about how hot it was, Luke put him in the freezer to cool off. The parrot was quiet for a while and then started screaming for help. Luke opened the door and the parrot wobbled out, profusely apologizing for being so obnoxious. Luke forgave him and the parrot leaned in close and whispered, "What did the chicken do?"

A man had a great berry patch. People came from far and wide to eat his berries. He eventually grew one fantastic berry that surpassed all the others. But one day a group of soldiers showed up at his door. He was afraid they were coming to take his prized berry so he opened the door slowly. The captain said, "Don't worry, we come not to seize your berry but to praise it." V93

Q: How can you tell if it's a dogwood?
A: By its bark.

Q: Why did the farmer want
to hear a cow sing?
A: It was moosic to his ears.

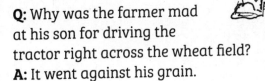

Q: Why was the farmer mad
at his son for driving the
tractor right across the wheat field?
A: It went against his grain.

Q: What happened when the Doves began to think
that they ruled the roost?
A: The Pigeons decided to stage a coo.

SUPER HARD ONE:
You are in space with two identical
bars of iron. One is a magnet, one is not.
How do you tell which is the
magnet? v94

"Thank goodness you arrived! I just talked to that rock over there for three hours, thinking it was you."

Appendix
Why are jokes funny?
(Perplex your parents!)

What makes a joke funny?

In this section, I try to explain _why a joke is funny_.

And it has homework for your parents.

What kind of joke does a toddler tell? Usually not very funny ones to persons older than four or five.

Like "The watermelon has legs." To a three- year-old, this is hilarious. They understand humor at a very elementary level. They understand that _what makes something funny is a surprise_. For example, a watermelon has legs!

That's true in general. A joke is funny because the punch line is unexpected or exaggerated. A Surprise. A change in direction from where you thought you were going.

To do that, you have to establish a direction—so there's the *rule of threes*.

There are usually *two misdirections that point you one way, and then a third rapid change.* Or two not funny statements and then a punch line that refers back to the first two.

Example:

A neutron, an electron, and a proton walk into a restaurant. (Three parts of an atom!)

After dinner, the (1) *electron gets his bill, and the* (2) *proton gets her bill, but the waiter says to the neutron, "No charge!"* (1, 2, punch line)

To tell a really good joke, you have to direct someone down one path and then switch direction with them.

This does something else—it creates tension. The listener is waiting for the punch line but can't see the destination. You create more tension with each piece of information that you give.

The neutron can walk into a French restaurant. Now is the punch line going to be about something to do with France? What did they eat? Was there nice atmosphere?

You can drag a joke out for 10 minutes—which just makes the listener tenser. A small punch line along the way may make people laugh, and then really laugh when the real punch line comes along.

For instance—

A tall electron, a short proton, and a round neutron ambled into a French restaurant with elegant atmosphere. The waiter seated them, but the electron and the proton switched to adjacent seats because they were attracted to each other.

They ordered three entrees: snails, frogs legs, and a hot dog. They couldn't eat all of it, so they asked the waiter to baguette.

Finally the waiter brought the bills. $23 for the proton, $31 for the electron and, turning to the neutron, he said, "No charge."

So you see—

Three characters, three dishes, lots of extraneous information to mislead (called a red herring, first said by William Cobbett in 1805, to describe dragging a salted herring around to mislead hounds) and finally, three punch lines.

You could go back and look at some of the simpler jokes in this book and write out a more complicated setup and tell the longer joke to the folks in the Front Seat.

How to tell a joke

— It's better if you don't announce that it is a joke. Just start right in.

— Do not start laughing.

— Do not snort milk through your nose while laughing.

— Don't ask if someone has "heard this one." If they haven't, they'll be glad to hear it. And if they have, they'll probably enjoy hearing it again.

— Don't tell jokes that are meant to hurt others. They may poke fun at all our mutual failings but should not be used to make someone else feel bad.

Tell jokes to the front seat (adults).

I assume you are not driving and you are in the back seat.

So, try to tell jokes to the people in the front seat (or adults anywhere in your life). You may not get the jokes, but hopefully they will.

Try this one:

I recently went to a party. There was a line to get in and a line for food, but there was no punch line. This is also a good one to expand.

This is funny because you set it up about the long lines for two things at the party, and then the third thing uses the same word with a different meaning. Rule of threes. But what makes it great is that it is a joke about jokes. It *has* a punch line, but *says* it doesn't.

This next joke breaks the rule of threes but has the same meaning switch with TWO words: "flies" and "like."

Time flies like an arrow.
Fruit flies like a banana.

Try it out on the adults.

V94: Let them stew for a long time.

They will try all sorts of things like, "The one with N and S printed on it" or "The one painted red with silver tips."

It's much more interesting than that.

A magnet has a magnetic field associated with it. This extends from the north end to the south, just like the earth.

A non-magnetized iron bar does not have this magnetic field. The greatest attraction for the field is at the ends.

So, if you were to hold the bars perpendicular and slowly move one bar from the tip of the other bar to its other end, if the stationary bar is a magnet, it will start out tugging at the bar and then release at the mid-point where forces are equal, and then be attracted again as you approach the other end.

If you switch positions, with the iron bar stationary, the magnet will be attracted the entire length of the iron bar.

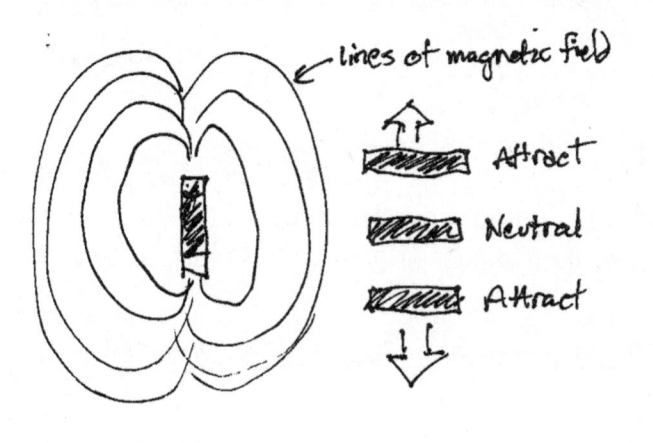

V85: The first letter of 1, 2, 3, 4, 5, 6, 7, 8, 9, 10, 11, 12, 13, 14, 15, 16, 17, 18, 19, and 20.

V86: These are all names of artists.

V87: Soapstone is a metamorphic rock that is very soft with a Mohs hardness of 1! You can easily carve it with a knife. It used to be used in chemistry labs as a countertop because it didn't react with chemicals. It does, however, feel soapy to the touch.

V88: The "Pulitzer Prize" is given each year for excellent writing. "Pullet" is another name for a young hen.

V89: "Cosines" are undulating waves in math; "porcine" sounds similar, but refers to pigs.

V90: Caesar Salad is romaine salad lettuce with croutons and a bunch of other stuff. It would be more appropriate if it were Roman lettuce rather than romaine, since it involves Caesar!

V91: This should be slipped into a series of "knock-knock jokes" (see pages 46-53 of this book) in a rapid sequence, so the other person immediately says "Knock Knock."

The silence after you say "Who's there?" is delightful. Savor the moment!

V92: Thoreau is pronounced "tho-row" which sounds like "throw."

Henry David Thoreau was a pre-Civil War thinker and writer. He wrote *Walden*, advocating a simple life, and *Civil Disobedience*, on how citizens can peacefully resist government.

V93: This is a twist on a line from Shakespeare's play, *Julius Caesar*—"I come to bury Caesar, not to praise him."

V80: "Cross my heart and hope to die."
Becomes: Hoss my creart and dope to hie.

"The early bird catches the worm."
Becomes: The barly eird watches the corm.

"Children should be seen and not heard."
Becomes: Shildren chould be heen and not seard.

"The darkest hour is just before dawn."
Becomes: The harkest dour is just defore bawn.

"To boldly go where no man has gone before."
Becomes: To goldly bo mere no whan has bone gefore.

"A picture is worth a thousand words."
Becomes: A wicture is porth a wousand thords.

"A nest of vipers."
Becomes: A vest of nipers.

"A rolling stone gathers no moss."
Becomes: A stolling rone mathers no goss.

"A dog is a man's best friend."
Becomes: A mog is a dan's frest biend.

V81: Author: A. H. Reginald Buller, a Canadian botany professor! "Relativity" says that time depends on your perspective, and that it's actually possible to travel in time at different speeds. So, returning the previous night would be a fun way to time travel. I love time travel.

V82: Carolyn Wells (1862-1942) wrote this in 1899.

V83: He arrived at home plate.

V84: Wow—these words sound different if capitalized!

V66: Use this carefully, or you may cause panic in the Front Seat. Best done while pulling off the exit to the rest stop.

V67: "Fast" means both "quickly"--and "holding off from eating."

V68: With global climate change, much of Florida is likely to be under water in your lifetime. Which is really not very funny.

V69: The silence after someone in the Front Seat says "When do we want it?" is delightful. This is one of my favorites.

V70: They are all synonyms.

V71: "A spare agus"—that is, an "extra one." Whatever an agus is...your gus is as good as mine.

V72: Scottish men play bagpipes and wear wool skirts called "kilts." It also sounds like the improper past tense of kill ("killed"), i.e. "kilt."

V73: Betty Reese.

V74: Oscar Wilde.

V75: Can you explain what this means?

V76: The sun rises in the east and sets in the west. Yeast makes the dough rise and after you eat it, it adds fat to your waist.

V77: There is no such thing as a "lert." But when you say the sentence out loud, it sounds like its referring to a "lert." It's fun to think of what a "lert" might be. What do you think?

V78: Goes to the hospital "Emergency Room" (ER).

V79: "Buccaneer" is another name for a pirate, which interestingly, is derived from someone who roasts meat, because of their barbeques! Those fun-loving pirates...

outstretched and fingers pointing down. (Animal is alive.) Then turn your hand over, pointing up. (Animal is dead.)

V55: Author: Karlos Moser. He didn't lie, nor did he offend the gift giver!

V56: Three punch lines in one joke! 1) They tell jokes so often they just say the number; 2) The guest didn't say the number well; and 3) A joke they had never heard before is defined only by the number--no joke told!

V57: A scale of "1:1" means it's the same size as the original.

V58: Author--Steve Hofmann (when he was in 2nd grade). Both things are true--a turkey is a like a large chicken, AND someone who is afraid is sometimes called a "chicken."

V59: Sounds like "moo shu pork" (stir fried pork, green onions, and mushrooms, wrapped in a thin pancake).

V60: Cinnamon sugar.

V61: Author: David Terrell. You'd have to drive all the way around the world, and come back to Memphis from the other side!

V62: "A lei" is a Hawaiian necklace of flowers. And there's a company in Plano, near Dallas, that makes Fritos (a type of corn chip) called "Frito Lay."

V63: They couldn't hear the "When do we want it?" because they need hearing aids!

V64: Procrastination means "to put things off until later." As in "Jimmy liked to procrastinate and do his homework at the last minute." (Don't be like Jimmy.)

V65: Because, if you can travel in time, it doesn't matter WHEN you get something! You can always travel to that time and get it! And remember, never do today what you can put off till tomorrow!

V43: "Hoarse."

V44: A photon is a packet of energy that is moving. It behaves as both a wave and a particle. That's not funny, just interesting. Light is a paradox.

V45: I "knew" you'd look this one up!

V46: The World Cup for soccer occurs every four years.

V47: If you are NOT an expert, then you are an amateur. But you can't be both an expert and an amateur.

V48: "I'll pack a lunch." The alpaca is closely related to the llama, though generally a bit smaller.

V49: Buildings are often made with two-by-four-inch pieces of lumber. "Tuba" sounds like "two by." (A two by four is actually 1½ × 3½ inches!) A "fermata" is a musical notation meaning you should hold a note as long as you want--which is what this workman was doing--taking as long as he wanted!

V50: The earth is rotating at about 1,000 mph, so it's always moving. But we're on it, so we don't notice. However, an "x" on a plane armrest won't help you to find that same spot later-- the plane is moving independently of everything else. Silliness all around!

V51: "Celery" sounds like "salary." He wanted a high salary.

V52: "Intense."

V53: A "juggler" is one who juggles. The "jugular vein" is a vulnerable spot in one's neck.

V54: Often, when an animal dies, we portray it with its legs pointing up in the air (because that often does happen when an animal dies). This joke can be done with your hands--if you want to show the joke to the Front Seat. Start with your hand

V32: A "platypus" is an aquatic mammal. Scottish people are known for wearing plaids. Get it?

V33: "Down" is the soft goose feathers that are used in pillows and comforters.

V34: This makes a pun on "yard"--a unit of measurement, and also a lawn around a house.

V35: "Raising cain" means "to cause trouble." On the other hand, "cane" is short for "sugarcane." (This would suggest that Adam and Eve were trouble-makers, because they raised Cain together.)

V36: "Metaphor" sounds like "meadow for." A *metaphor* is a figure of speech that implies a comparison as in "The backseat was a zoo." A *simile* compares one thing directly to a second thing, usually using the word "like" or "as." For instance, "This joke went over like a lead balloon."

V37: "Ten tickles" sounds like "tentacles." Tentacles are the long arms on an octopus.

V38: Pea, brownie, tea, buffet ("buff" is a yellow- brown).

V39: Doves make a sound called "cooing." A military rebellion is called a "coup," which sounds the same as "coo."

V40: The ending "who" doesn't fit all the s-words ahead of it, so the person answering doesn't know how to do "alliteration" (the stringing together of words that start with the same sound).

V41: Look at the white dots, and note that the dots around them are gray. But those dots turn white when your eye looks directly at them!

V42: This is actually a little misleading by having the question mark. Take the question mark away and then read it as a statement. Now it refers to the number of letters in each word. For instance, "What" = 4, etc.

V22: "Telekinesis" means "the ability to make something at a distance move without touching it." Joke is attributed to many, including Kurt Vonnegut.

V23: Dogs are often taught to follow closely behind the owner or "to heel." And that sounds like "heal," which is what a doctor does.

V24: A bench in a church is often called a "pew." This joke stinks.

V25: Of course, a whale is MUCH bigger than a tree.

V26: People used to travel with very large boxy suitcases called "trunks." No one does anymore, so you can be pretty sure this is an old joke.

V27: The moon has several phases, which describe how much of the moon is in shadow, e.g. full, crescent, new. The moon is illuminated by the sun—so what we are seeing is the "daytime" on the moon.

V28: "Current" means "recent." It also means "moving electrons that can shock you"!

V29: "Exit." Not "eggsactly" hilarious, but we "shell" see if there are any better "yolks" (jokes) to come.

V30: Canadians are known for adding an "eh?" to the end of their sentences.

Speaking of Canada, do you know how that country got its name? They put all the letters in a hat and then pulled them out, one by one.

C, eh? N, eh? D, eh?

V31: If your tooth hurts ("tooth hurty"), that sounds like "2:30."

V9 Lichens are a kind of "fungi"--which sounds like "Fun Guy."

V10: Often there are signs that warn that cars will be "towed."

V11: A mime is a person who conveys a story in silence, using no words.

V12: What Lincoln used to say was: "A man's legs must be long enough to reach the ground." (Imagine a president with humor like that!)

V13: Crabs walk sideways.

V14: Just air and space, which technically is not "nothing," but it's a joke. Relax! And it's a great museum.

V15: "Bovine" refers to cows, and it sounds like "vine."

V16: He sewed his hand on upside down.

V17: "One, Two, Three" in Spanish is "Uno, Dos, Tres." Note that "Tres" sounds like "trace."

V18: This is a great joke. It could be true both ways you read it. They no longer make yardsticks. OR--yardsticks are always the same length. It's a good one to say aloud to an older person (who probably used to use a yardstick) and wait for the double meaning to sink in.

V19: "Score" means the number of runs in baseball or, in music, it's the book with the music printed in it.

V20: "Without peer" means there is nothing that is comparable. "Piers" are raised structures extending into the ocean. They sound the same!

V21: "Meteor" sounds like "meat eater."

The Vault

V1: 12 is a dozen, 144 is a gross, and 288 is "two" gross.

V2: "Range" can mean "stove"—or "wild expanses" out West.

V3: "Framed" can mean a painting is placed in a frame; or "framed" can mean that someone improperly led others to believe that an innocent person committed a crime. The Mona Lisa is one of the world's most famous paintings.

V4: Atoms have protons (+), electrons (-), and neutrons (no charge). When atoms lose an electron, they have a net positive charge.

V5: The Roman numeral for 3,000 is one thousand (M) three times or MMM.

V6: An "imposter" is someone who pretends to be something they're not. Noodles are a form of pasta. "Impasta" sounds like "imposter."

V7: This means innately knowing how to do something. But it sounds like "stink" which is what skunks often do.

V8: They lack toes. This is funny because milk has lactose as an ingredient.

About the Author

Jobo is another name for Jay B. Parrish, PhD, a geophysicist in real life. He has always loved jokes.

When he was 10, he signed his name on a letter to the Pennsylvania Geological Survey with a quill pen and much flourish. The result:

The staff wrote back, "Dear JoBo." The name stuck.

Jay enjoys jokes and riddles with his wife Marilyn, his children, and especially with his young grandchildren.

For more information about this book and other titles published by Walnut Street Books, please visit **www.walnutstreetbooks.com**.